Free the Trapped Soul

(Delivered and Set Free)

Gary Walker, Jr.

Free the Trapped Soul… (Delivered and Set Free)

Copyright © 2019 by Gary Walker

All rights reserved. No part of this book may be reproduced or transmitted in any form or by any means without written permission of the author.

Published by Kingdom Kaught Publishing, LLC
Denton, Maryland USA
Printed in the USA

Library of Congress Control Number: 2016956328

ISBN 9780996404051

DEDICATION

First and foremost, I give thanks to my Lord and Savior, Jesus the Christ, whom all praises are due, and giving honor for His grace and mercy. Thanking God for my praying wife the Evangelistic Pastor Wannetta Ann Walker, the best lady in my life, my grandmother, Jenieve Walker (God rest her soul), and my Aunt Debbie Poole for all her support throughout my whole life.

My soul looks back and wonders how I got over……

Acknowledgments

I give thanks to my Spiritual Leaders and Friends:

Prophet Dr. Dewey Rowe
Dewey Rowe Ministries

Pastor Gerald Carpenter
Annapolis Church of God

Bishop Craig Coates
Fresh Start Ministries

Pastor Charles Carroll
New Creation Deliverance Ministries

Prophet Sandra McCulough
Christ Ministries Inc.

Bishop Charles S. Waters
New Generation Ministries

Pastor Dr. Pamela W. Hicks
The Awakening Grace Ministries

And a special thanks to some good friends in Christ, Bishop Livingston Roll, Pastor Butch Acklin, Bishop Antonio Palmer, Minister William Spruill, and Frank Butler.

I pray that God will bless the readers of these words. As you read: Free The Trapped Soul, I pray that you can find yourself within the pages and find just what God has been trying to tell you about yourself or even equip you to help others. I know that God will give you the insight to find yourself in each chapter and or a situation that you can relate to in your life. And understand that God wants to use you in the Kingdom building process.

There have been times in our lives that we faced a lot of tricks of the devil and we are still standing because of God's grace and mercy. Please read this with an open heart and mind, growing towards spiritual maturity in Christ Jesus.

To Grow in Christ Jesus:

Prayer:

In the Name of Jesus, first and foremost I give You thanks for giving me one more day, and God today I decided not to be the person I was yesterday, but to act as a (man/woman) and not as a child any more. I pray Lord God to be spiritually mature in You and put away childish things. I declare and decree to walk the faith walk in love in order for You my God to grow in and through me. I am an overcomer with You, God, I have defeated Satan and my past, and I will not be defeated in unforgiveness, envy, jealousy or resentment. I thank God the Father for Your grace and mercy, that You made available for me, through Your Son Jesus the Christ and I thank You. Amen

Confession:

In the Name of Jesus and by the power of the Holy Spirit, I will give You, God, all the honor that is do Your Name, for the glory of every good thing that has happened in my life, and I will sing to the Lord a new song, sing to the Lord all the earth. (Psalm 96:1-2) I declare that I am more than a conqueror! My Faith, My Joy and My Love is rising in the mighty Name of Jesus. Amen.

Table of Contents

Chapter 1 - Playing the Shame Game 1

Chapter 2 - You Are Not Good Enough 17

Chapter 3 - Are You Set Free? 25

Chapter 4 - Why God? 39

Chapter 5 - Living Among Confusion 47

Chapter 6 - Detachment through True Repentance 53

Chapter 7 - Falling in Love with Lies 63

Chapter 8 - Being Raised from the Dead 71

Chapter 9 - Lacking Faith and the Power Thereof! 77

Chapter 10 - Reaping the Benefits 87

Chapter 11 Thank God for His Grace and Mercy 93

Chapter 1

Playing the Shame Game

In 1979, I, Gary Walker Jr., made the argument that my life was trapped and my soul needed to be free. I had a false pretense that alcohol and drugs would free me. What I am about to share with you concerning addiction is that it is not a disease, but it is a bondage. To prove my point about addiction, let me form a distinction between the word 'disease' and the word 'bondage.' And share my own experiences in dealing with addiction to let you decide what you are dealing with today. First let us clear up the word, addiction; it's not just pertaining to drugs. Addiction is anything that has you bound, such as men, women, the love of money, sex, other people's mates, etc.

Now that we cleared that up, let's discuss bondage and disease. Bondage is labor or service (of a servant or a slave that has you connect to it). Disease is a pathological condition of the mind or body. What is the difference between the two? One, you do not have to work to maintain it, and the other one must work and labor to keep it. What I want you, the reader, to understand is that a disease is something that you catch; it's something we did not bring upon ourselves by our own actions. It exists in the body and needs nothing to stay there. On the other hand, bondage requires effort to maintain. It is a heavy burden and causes one to become a slave to his desires, which fits the definition of bondage, perfectly.

Why are you in a state of bondage? That is the first thing you need to know. Let me tell you how I answered this question. In 1982, I made drugs, women, alcohol, and parties my Pharaoh; I became a slave to my own fleshly desires. These things destroyed me; I got to be real with you, open and honest. Even after my ordination, I was still struggling with the trapped soul in my flesh. Did the drugs have me in bondage or was it something else?

Throughout my studies of addiction, desires, and disease what I found to be the most troubling problem is that we are created of flesh, and most of all spirit. Remember I'm not just saying addiction is all drug related; it is whatever may be holding you in bondage.

Chapter 1 - Playing the Shame Game

My theory is that addiction is not a disease; it is a spiritual bondage. Pause a moment and reflect on what I just said. Desires are the effects and not the cause of something greater happening in the person's life and that something is spiritual bankruptcy. Spiritual bankruptcy is what happens in the life of an individual when he or she believes that they are nothing, worthless, no good, flawed, and less the human. The only thing flawed is their thinking! In error, they believe nothing can help them. I use to feel like that growing up in a broken home with a family member telling me that I would be nothing.

And I accepted the idea of being worthless. When people accept that belief, it signifies emptiness inside. When something that is supposed to be full becomes empty, the natural thing to do is to try to fill the void. Desire is an attachment to an object in an attempt to fill the barren life with pleasure and joy. My belief is that the person in bondage is attached to an object that creates a deceptive spiritual experience, which produces an emotional or pleasurable feeling that has only temporary results. This is why breaking away from desires of the flesh is impossible through human interventions (medicine, therapy, counseling and such) because man has not within him the means to fill a spiritually empty life. This book is designed to eliminate addictions, desires and bondage. I do not believe in the old saying, "once bound always bound." The devil is a liar!

What is the ordinary truth that Israel fails to see? They failed to see that they were powerless over their enemies without God. Just like you and I, they were powerless over fleshly desires. The person in bondage cannot overcome without God. If you have admitted to yourself that you cannot defeat your desires, you are not ready for a miracle and, you will be defeated by your worldly desires. Powerless means doing things that are out of God's Will. If we cannot stop then why do we believe that we are in control? Fleshly desire is a controlling power over our life. Only God can break the power of worldly desires and bondage because it is a spiritual force that we have allowed to take hold of our lives. Our inability to control our desires is a system of spiritual bondage. If you cannot accept the idea that you are powerless over your fleshly desires then you are like Israel attempting to overcome an enemy with your own strength. If you cannot accept this idea then you might as well remain a slave because you are not ready for God to help you. You still believe you are in control of you own life!

Chapter 1 - Playing the Shame Game

We are responsible for our own salvation, because by our own choice (free will) we open the door to those overpowering forces. Likewise, we are responsible for our deliverance for by our own choice we must turn to God and ask for His help. As much as you want to live right in your power, you cannot; all men and women face this problem.

Romans 8:1-7

"There is therefore now no condemnation to them which are in Christ Jesus, who walk not after the flesh, but after the Spirit. For the law of the Spirit of life in Christ Jesus hath made me free from the law of sin and death. For what the law could not do, in that it was weak through the flesh, God sending his own Son in the likeness of sinful flesh, and for sin, condemned sin in the flesh: That the righteousness of the law might be fulfilled in us, who walk not after the flesh, but after the Spirit. For they that are after the flesh do mind the things of the flesh; but they that are after the Spirit the things of the Spirit. For to be carnally minded is death; but to be spiritually minded is life and peace. Because the carnal mind is enmity against God: for it is not subject to the law of God, neither indeed can be."

Free the Trapped Soul

You cannot live right (righteous) without God. You need His help and power to do so. Therefore, God sent Jesus, His Son, to give us the power by destroying sin in our flesh. If you stay with God, you will be okay, but if you walk away living life based on your own terms, you will fail. I was one who walked away and many times fell flat on my butt in shame. I was ashamed of certain people in my family and even ashamed of myself. Shame is a painful state of awareness of one's basic defectiveness as a human being.

This is probably going to be the most painful, but the most important part of your journey, because in essence it deals with your pain. Before I could even begin to write this, God helped me to deal with shame and held me when I cried. A sense of failure is a central characteristic for the individual who experiences shame. The deficit is internal for the shamed person; it is felt as a failure of being. The person feels inadequate as a human being, as if, when born God had made a mistake in creating such a flawed and defective organism. The shame crisis is spiritual in that a shamed individual questions the reason for his life, often finding no justification for his existence. He or she believes that he / she is less than fully human.

Chapter 1 - Playing the Shame Game

Someone experiencing shame senses that he is falling far short of his goals in life. These expectations are not necessarily moral or ethical. They may be related to his career, family, or even appearance. They often reflect parental expectations. Shame occurs whenever something happens that forces the person to notice the gap between his actual performance and those expectations. For example, a man who has grown up with "macho" beliefs may be humiliated by temporary impotence; a sexual disappointment that he believes signifies that he is really a sexual fraud. He may also believe that everyone can see his weakness, and that they hold him in utter contempt. This is exactly what Adam and Eve experienced in the Garden of Eden, and this is where it all began with Sin. Two key words 'expectations and parents' play a major role in why so many people struggle with internal shame. The questions that you must answer are what did or what didn't someone do to me that made me more aware of my defects than God and His mercy? Who told me that I was naked, that I don't measure up, that somehow I am inadequate?

Twenty years ago I had one of those life-jolting discoveries that significantly changed everything I named the core demon in my life. I named it "Shame"; naming shame means that I became aware of the massive destructive power that shame had exerted in my life. I discovered that I had been bound by shame all my life. It ruled me like an addiction. I acted it out; I covered it up in subtle and not so subtle ways. I transferred it to my family, my children and the people I taught.

What is shame? Shame carries with it the thought of humiliation and represents the feeling of public disgrace; it means to wound, dishonor, disgrace, nakedness or broken spirit. This is what happens to our spirits when we enter into shame. Shame is an inner sickness or a disease of the soul, and expresses itself through inner torment. The emotional pain associated with shame comes from what we believe to be true about ourselves, whether or not it is true or false.

There is a difference between guilt and shame. Shame can come from failing to live up to certain standards; guilt results from breaking rules. Shame is rooted in a feeling that we are somehow defective; guilt is related to a mistake that has been made. Guilt relates to behavior; shame relates to one's very identity. Guilt is felt for making a mistake; shame is felt for *being* a

Chapter 1 - Playing the Shame Game

mistake. Shame was the unconscious demon I had never acknowledged. In becoming aware of the dynamics of shame, I came to see that shame is one of the major destructive forces in all human life. In naming shame I began to have power over it.

Toxic shame is experienced as the attitude that I am flawed and defective as a human being. Shame is no longer an emotion that signals our limits, it is a state of being (an identity). The person suffering from toxic shame is dying, internally. Toxic shame gives one a sense of worthlessness, a sense of failing and falling short as a human being. Toxic shame is a rupture of the self with the self, to the self. In toxic shame the person becomes an object of disgrace, and object that cannot be trusted. As an object that can't be trusted, one experiences oneself as untrustworthy. There is shame about shame. People will readily admit quilt, hurt or fear before they will admit shame. What we are talking about here is shame as an identity. Any human emotion can become internalized. When internalized, an emotion stops functioning in the manner of an emotion and becomes a way of acting, a lifestyle.

Free the Trapped Soul

The problem of toxic shame is ultimately a spiritual problem. Spirituality is the essence of human existence. We are not material beings on a spiritual journey; we are spiritual beings who need an earthly journey to become fully spiritual. Spirituality is about being, and being is about why there is something, rather than nothing. To be truly human is to have an inner self and a life from within. When humans no longer have an inner life, they become deprived of human qualities such as individuality, compassion, politeness or civility. Toxic shame looks to the outside for happiness and for validation, since the inside is flawed and defective. Toxic shame is spiritual bankruptcy.

As I mentioned before, I was ashamed of my parents who were both extremely socially inept. They were crude, unable to express love, except to their mates, and I could say pets, upon which they lavished excessive affection. I was embarrassed by them and, yet instinctively I knew I should not feel this way. I knew I should have loved and respected my parents, so I was tormented in that area as well. I can recall one particularly bad incident in which my mother embarrassed me, greatly. As a little boy, about ten years old, I was invited to a Thanksgiving dinner, and I refused

Chapter 1 - Playing the Shame Game

to eat some sweet potatoes. It set my mother off and she began to curse like a sailor in front of everybody! She started beating me with a belt then a broomstick. I was stunned as I saw people's jaws drop in disbelief, but somehow they found humor in it. I was mortified!

A child who grows up in a normal household will receive a mixture of verbal and non-verbal messages that eventually help guide him towards knowing when, where and how he can properly exhibit himself to the world. She will get enough attention so that she can conclude that although she may not always be at the center of her world she certainly has a proper place in it. He expects regularly that he will be the primary focus of his or her parents' attention, both in many small ways every day, and at least occasionally for big events like birthdays and Christmases. He learns to expect that his parents love him and approve of what they see.

Unfortunately, not all family systems provide this support for the developing child. Sometimes parents do not seem capable of sparing any positive attention, perhaps because they met with little themselves. Members of these families mostly speak out messages that tell the child he or she is not good or not good enough. Children raised in these shame-bound families tend to internalize their parents' disapproval. They become "shamed based," feeling deep shame at the core of their beings. The crucial fear for these children is that of abandonment and of death by emotional starvation. After all they are just learning that the world does not revolve around them, that they have wants and needs which they cannot meet themselves. Their universe has become a more dangerous place, one in which they cannot be certain of survival. Abandonments may be physical or emotional, neglected or abusive. The common denominator is that these youth realize that any love or affection they get from their family can be withdrawn, perhaps suddenly. The child may eventually conclude that he is basically unlovable.

The fear of abandonment they feel cannot be alleviated because they no longer ask themselves whether or not they will be abandoned, but only how and when. Abandonment becomes a certainty to deeply shamed individuals. However, they will probably continue to quest after love in all the wrong places and with the wrong people. I had to realize the way to decrease my fear of abandonment was by identifying with and incorporating positive goals and ideas in me.

Chapter 1 - Playing the Shame Game

Likewise, the more children tend to develop a more realistic concept of their desired selves, the more this will help them become independent individuals. They can challenge themselves to become their ideal type of parents. They can feel pride rather than shame about themselves because they have internalized a sense of approval from their nurturer, Jesus Christ.

In dealing with shame I had a self-esteem issue, like a lot of you. The value of self-esteem lies not in the fact that it allows us to feel better, but that it allows us to live better, to respond to challenges and opportunities more resourcefully and more appropriately. Healthy self-esteem equates with rationality, realism, perception, creativity, independence, flexibility, adaptability, humility, kindness, optimism, and cooperation. Poor self-esteem equates with irrationally, blindness to reality, inability to manage change (inflexibility), unwillingness to admit or correct mistakes, stubbornness, fear of the new and unfamiliar, inappropriate conformity, rebelliousness, defensiveness, negativity, over-complaining, or over-controlling behavior, and fear of or hostility towards others.

Free the Trapped Soul

I believed the lie that I was stupid for many for many years. I thought I was an idiot, a person with a low IQ, who would never amount to much more in life than working in the most menial jobs. I just thought I didn't have the smarts for a real job. This belief went back to the second and third grades, when an abusive teacher called me stupid nearly every day and often threaten me with no recess or even detentions. Eventually, I believed and decided never to study or try to please any teachers again. I believed in my heart that teachers were the enemy. I also thought I was just too damn dumb to learn from them. Years later I graduated from high school with a C minus average. I wasn't proud of it, but I believed it was justly deserved. I was stupid, so I got what I deserved.

But then something happened I accepted Christ at the age of 40 seriously. Until then I had played church, with all my issues of drugs, a bad marriage, imprisonment, and homelessness. But I'm glad God had a plan for me.

The Lord called me to learn more of Him, and to attend Bible College to prepare to do His work. I remember telling the Lord, "Why me, God, I'm too stupid, I have a speech problem; God, why?" God spoke to my heart, 'I will go with you, I will help you.' That, of course, was truth. The Lord never left me and it's based on His Word in the book of Hebrews 13:5 "Let your conversation be without covetousness; and be content with such things as ye have; for he hath said, I will never leave thee, nor forsake thee." Hearing those words in my heart was an astonishing moment of hope, charged with faith, something I'd rarely experienced! I decided to take God up on it, even though I did have some serious doubts about my abilities. Again I was amazed God might want someone like me in His work! In fact, I couldn't find anyone in the Bible I considered as dumb as me, so in many ways none of this made sense to me. Why did He want me? One day, through always looking for some proof that I was wrong, I happened to read Psalm 139:14 "I am fearfully and wonderfully made." For a moment I sat down in awe of God's Word to me, and then I simply thought 'Okay, if He says so, I'll accept it.' With vigor, peace of mind and a flow of warmth entered my heart. I can never forget that day, because from that day on, the problem of my intellect was solved. I was no longer an addict, and my strongholds were lifted.

Chapter 2

You Are Not Good Enough

Let's go back to the time before you and I found God. Here is where others that matter the most, *may* tell children that they have some worth, *but* that they continue to fall short of their goals. Family members focus on an idealized version of acceptable performance and expected perfection. Often a child gets compared to the sibling who is more successful. (Your sister got straight A's again.) This comparison lets the child know that he or she is somewhat of a disappointment and inadequate.

Yes, I heard those old phrases 'You are just like your father, no damn good; you make me sick!' I couldn't say or do anything right or even good enough for my mother. And my father would always shoot down my dreams with statements like: 'Boy you are too dumb for college and we don't have money to waste on you.' The funny thing about that is my parents let my grandparents raised me. The shame trapped with these messages is that no matter how hard the person tries to become good enough, no matter what that person does, they remain a disappointment to others and ultimately to him or herself. He must endlessly quest for approval. The mottos in his life become "What more do you want from me?" "How can I please you?" and "What more can I do for you?"

Just as I felt, I understand how you may be feeling, and maybe how you address your children or even family members. The "you are not good enough" message could cause one to conclude that it is useless to continue to seek goals of approval since he or she is destined for failure. Sometimes he or she will do just that, but to do so may feel to them like admitting total failure. They will then encounter shame of not being good enough and the shame of not being good at all. The meaning of life is in the search for approval from others; giving up the search is crushing and doubles the shame.

Nor can the person of the "you are not good enough" message simply fail quickly at some task then go on to succeed, elsewhere. They must repeat the pattern of almost succeeding in everything in their life,

Chapter 2 - You Are Not Good Enough

particularly in those areas defined by family as critical for self-worth. They must try hard and never relax. I even fell into the "you don't belong" category in which others told me that they had some valuable characteristics that set them apart from me. Is there anything in you that sets you apart from others? If you cannot find it, I'll tell you it's the God in you.

The recipient of the "you do not belong" message often feels a mixture of loneliness and shame. Although our flaws may not be central to the family as that "no-good" child, nevertheless it is too serious to be forgotten, the stigma, a visible or invisible mark that can't be ignored. The sense of these messages may be that God had made a terrible or subtle mistake in creating this damaged individual. This child (or even yourself) does not fit in with the family. We are outcasts, strangers. Others may not even recognize that they are estranged. I used to feel this way in my family, and later in other groups. I started to believe I was different. These differences may appear trivial, but they are not. Some felt that I was too short, with a funny-shaped head, red-hair, a little too intelligent, or not intelligent enough.

Free the Trapped Soul

Whenever possible, we may attempt to conform to the expectations and norm of the groups to whom we yearn to belong. I became that person so expert on wearing a mask in attempts to hide my unacceptable traits from my family, friends, and even from myself. I'd try to conform in areas of thoughts, values, appearance, and behavior. Nevertheless, I would never believe that I really belonged. My position in life was that of the person I was, forever watching others, wishing I could belong with a group, but knowing I couldn't. The individual who cannot belong may be filled with a sense of longing. "If only….", "If I was better looking," "if only I could figure out what more to do." Or "if only I could do enough," but early experiences of failure prevent this person from being able to join in wholeheartedly even when, later in life, opportunities arise. Full from shame, we as individuals who did not belong become certain that we cannot belong and suffer a bitter life of separation.

Romans 9:17-23

"For the scripture saith unto Pharaoh, even for this same purpose have I raised thee up, that I might shew my power in thee, and that my name might be declared throughout all the earth.

Chapter 2 - You Are Not Good Enough

Therefore hath he mercy on whom he will have mercy, and whom he will he hardened. Thou wilt say then unto me, why doth he yet find fault? For who hath resisted his will? Nay but, O man, who art thou that replies against God? Shall the thing formed say to him that formed it, why hast thou made me thus? Hath not the potter power over the clay, of the same lump to make one vessel unto honour, and another unto dishonour? What if God, willing to shew his wrath, and make his power known, endured with much longsuffering the vessel of wrath fitted to destruction: And that he might make known the riches of his glory on the vessels of mercy, which he had afore prepared unto glory."

To have low self-esteem is to feel inappropriate to life; wrong; not about this issue or that, but wrong as a person. To have average self-esteem is to fluctuate between feeling appropriate and inappropriate. To have high self-esteem is to feel confidently appropriate to life. The ultimate source of self-esteem is and can only be internal, in what we do, not what others do or think about us. When we seek it in externals, in actions and response of others, we invite tragedy into our lives.

Sometimes I felt I was not lovable. Fear of abandonment is a central theme in shame. It is vital to remember that many children are emotionally or physically abandoned, because of their parents' inability, disinterest or distractions. Other children are not abandoned but are subjected to repeated verbal or non-verbal messages that they are essentially unlovable, like I used to feel. The reason I felt like that (and maybe you) is because being unlovable may be entirely unpredictable. For instance, a child may have the misfortune to remind a parent of a particularly unattractive relative. Another child may be of the wrong sex, as when a single mother who cannot tolerate men must raise a boy. Perhaps parental child bonding never occurred at birth. Whatever the reason, these children learn that they are extra baggage in their families. I felt like an old traveling bag that would get used and tossed in the corner after the trip.

The person who believes he is unlovable feels deep shame. We may believe that he or she is beneath notice, not worth somebody else's time or energy. They may feel contempt for themselves. We, and I say, "We" because I am not exempt from this. We may be dismayed and confused since we cannot know exactly why we have been put on earth, when we are unworthy. As an adult, we have great difficulty accepting love from others. At best we will believe that love or caring directed towards each other is a result of misjudgment on the part of the sender, at worst we will disdainfully reject caring, unable to respect anyone who cannot see that we are unworthy.

The individual who grows up feeling essentially unlovable may become a "caretaker," somebody who devotes their life to caring for others. This is a way to deflect the pain of being unlovable in one's own right. Caretakers argue that the only meaningful thing they can do with their lives is to give to others. They consider themselves unworthy of receiving pleasure, love or admiration. The way they can belong is by giving to those who are lovable. At the same time they may suffer periods of despair when they plaintively ask "why doesn't anyone about my needs?" The unlovable person does not necessarily give up the desire to be loved, only the idea that they never will be. But I am a living witness that you are lovable in many aspects of your life. Never give up on God, because He never gives up on you.

Chapter 3

Are You Set Free?

Demonic spirits are evil personalities. These spirits had me running away from a good home of loving people to a house that was full of demon spirits. I even would run and hide in the woods, because I often wanted to die. At the age of ten, I did not want to go on at all because demon spirits had taken over my thoughts. It is important that we become a people of freedom, suffering not to the things of this world. The trouble we all faced at one point and time in our life arises out of a false notion of disease. Medical people (along with the whole of our society) think there is only one basic kind of disease, whereas in fact there are three. There is not only physical but also mental and spiritual disease; and they cannot be fixed with the same bag of tools. Yes, the only disease I had was in my spirit. Spiritual disease must be dealt with spiritually; otherwise a person cannot be set free. The main components of the spirit are intelligence, will and passion, and it is exactly here that the person is essentially sick or stuck in bondage.

Free the Trapped Soul

My spirit was sick of being (and like some of you) I felt that life would be better somewhere else. We need to recover and in order to recover from a spiritual disease we must speak to the spirit, and our spirits must obey the Holy Spirit. Obedience is the key. All disorder, and all disease, arises when natural superiors fail to rule and natural subordinates fail to obey. Therefore, a man's body should obey his soul, and when it doesn't, physical disease results. A man's soul should obey his spirit, and when it doesn't mental disease results. A man's spirit should obey God and when it doesn't, spiritual disease results. Now it is a fact that every attempt to correct the spiritual disease by manipulation of man's lower principles results only in an endless circle of inconclusive results.

Demons are spirits that are revealed through behaviors. Their objectives in human beings are to tempt, deceive, accuse, condemn, pressure, defile, resist, oppose, control, steal, afflict, kill and destroy. They are enemies of God and man. Demons enter through open doors; they have to be given an opportunity. There must be an opening through which we have allowed Satan to enter. Let's look at what Satan told Eve: that 'once you

Chapter 3 - Are You Set Free?

know good and evil, you will be free to make your own decisions.' You will no longer be dependent on God. There are three ways that man has sought independence from God since the fall of Adam and Eve: science, religion and material gain.

The desire to be independent of God is the distinctive mark of all who belong to the kingdom of Satan: rebellious angels, demons and fallen humanity. So long as man remains in submission to God and his soul remains in submission to his spirit, man's function is in harmony with God and himself. But if at any time man reasserts his rebellion against God, his soul is no longer in submission to his spirit and the inner harmony is broken. Mine was a case of spiritual emptiness. I had to realize that all Christians died with Christ, so all Christians have been freed from sin. If they don't believe they're free from sin, they'll probably not live like it. We act according to our belief. The central issue is always identity. If you don't know the truth about your identity in Christ; it doesn't make any difference what people say. Spiritual strongholds use up desires. It is like a psychic cancer, sucking our life energy into specific obsessions and compulsions leaving less and less life available for our children, family, loved ones and other pursuits. The woman of Samaria was empty of life. She had lost her ability to love and had come to a place where she believed that it was hopeless for her.

John 4:11

"The woman saith onto him, Sir thou hast nothing to draw with, and the well is deep: from whence then hast thou that living water?"

Strongholds suck all of our strength to live out of us and cause us to lose hope. As the woman of Samaria discovered, we must also come to see in this group that there is no well too deep for God to heal. No pain, heartache, failure, or sickness that Jesus Christ cannot heal. Jesus offered her living water so that she would never thirst again. Today, it is that same spirit that He offers to quench our thirst and fill us with everlasting Life. To be truly human is to have an inner life, a life from within. The devil dwells in dry places. The woman at the well represented thirst; what she needed is not what she wanted.

Chapter 3 - Are You Set Free?

The American Heritage & Webster Dictionary defines craving and thirst to be actually the same thing: they both are desires.

Craving - A fervent wish for what promises gratification: desire, appetence, appetite, craving, hunger, itch, longing, lust thirst, urge, yearning, yen, hankering, and hungriness.

Thirst - A fervent wish for what promises gratification: desire, appetence, appetite, craving, hunger, itch, longing, lust thirst, urge, yearning, yen, hankering, and hungriness.

Her craving is actually a thirst. Her desire for men and sex is an attempt to fill a void in her life. She is empty inside. The well is too deep. She believes that there is no hope for her. She sought fulfillment and pleasure from things outside of herself (men). It is really, not about, what she wants driving her strongholds; it's about what she lacks and needs. Jesus offers her Living Water that she may never thirst again.

The craving, that the person in spiritual strongholds experiences, is actually a thirst for the Spirit of God in his life. The stronghold craving is a thirst to replace the missing life, joy, peace and love that is not there. Jesus offers water to the woman to quench her thirst forever. In other words, Jesus is saying 'change who or whatever you turn to for pleasure, turn to Me, and I will break the craving (strongholds). I will quench your thirst.

This is the point; her true desire was not for men and sex or whatever; her true desire was for God. But for some reason in her life the woman turned away from God and her true desire, and chose out of her own free will to crave men and other strongholds.

Believe it or not in my spiritual emptiness, I was always angry. The Bible says in Ephesians 4:26-27, "And don't sin by letting anger gain control over you, don't let the sun go down while you are still angry, for anger gives a mighty foothold to the devil." Yes, I have had that same problem of anger. There were several times throughout the Old Testament where God has gotten angry. For example, Moses missed out on the Promised Land because of his disobedience when he struck the rock instead of speaking to it as God commanded him. God was very angry at Moses when He failed to obey

Chapter 3 - Are You Set Free?

Him. But because of the grace and mercy of Jesus the Christ, we can still see the promises of God, only through repentance for our sin, even the sin we committed through allowing anger to get the best of us.

Have there been times in your life (just like me) where you have been so angry that you sought out, or even plotted revenge against your sister/ brother? If you say 'no I never!' The devil is a liar. Praises be to God that we can fall to our knees and repent for even our thoughts.

You may say it's hard, but the Bible tells us if we want to be forgiven from our short-comings then we must forgive others of theirs. The Bible doesn't tell us that we shouldn't feel anger or get angry, but it points out that it is important to handle our anger, properly. If vented thoughtlessly, anger can hurt others and destroy relationships. If bottled up inside, it can cause you to become bitter and destroy yourself from within.

The Apostle Paul tells us to deal with our anger immediately in a way that builds relationships rather than destroy them. If we nurse anger, we will give Satan an opportunity to divide us. Are you angry with someone right now? What can you do to resolve your differences? Don't let the day end before you begin to work on mending your relationship! We can bring sorrow to the Holy Spirit by the way we live. Apostle Paul warns us against unwholesome language, bitterness, improper use of anger, harsh words, slander, and a bad attitude towards others in the state of anger.

Act in love towards your brothers and sisters in Christ, just as God acted in love by sending His Son to die for our sins. Are you bringing sorrow, or pleasing God with your attitude and actions? Instead of acting out, act in a way of forgiveness just as God has forgiven us. Our lives will have us living life in a pig pen with pride and anger. We lack the knowledge concerning God's Will and our purpose for life that leads to a life of self-centeredness.

Hosea 4:6

"My people are destroyed for lack of knowledge: because thou hast rejected knowledge, I will also reject thee, that thou shalt be no priest to me: seeing thou hast forgotten the law of thy God, I will also forget thy children."

Chapter 3 - Are You Set Free?

God has a plan and a way to live life, which is called the Word of God. Most of us grew up not knowing or understanding the purpose of Scripture and therefore a lack of knowledge lead us to live life on our own terms. A lot of us love to live life on our own terms and in our own ways. Self-centeredness is about my way; God-centeredness understands that God created you and has a purpose and plan for your life. In self-centeredness a lot of mistakes and failures are experienced in our lives because of our choice to live outside of God's Will. We need to understand that we are powerless over our circumstances. Remember that I said you are powerless over the demons of anger. I'm going to change that idea now and rephrase it this way, 'Human beings hate to appear weak and powerless before other human beings.' However, the shame associated with our inability to overcome anger on the spot is humiliating, so we keep trying to prove to everyone how strong we are. Our inability to overcome anger does just the opposite; it shows everyone how weak we are. Here's a sad joke, "Satan knows that you are spiritually bound by his demons, but you don't. So he laughs while you keep trying to get up on your own strength, and fail because you are powerless against him."

Free the Trapped Soul

The Jewish people in the text had developed a religion of negatives. They had taken a lot of things out of their lives, but what had they put in the place of them? What Jesus was saying to them is that if they did not put something positive in their lives after eliminating so many negative things, they would be like a man delivered of demons that did not put anything positive in his life. They would end up in a worse condition than they were in when they started. There must always be a balance between the positive and negative factors. After the flesh is crucified and demons are cast out, we must rely on Jesus. In fact, the reason for getting rid of demons is in order to be able to have more Jesus. To be filled with Jesus is to be filled with purity and power. For each demon cast out, the gift and fruits of the Spirit must replace it. The gifts represent power and the fruit represent purity. It is not enough to just ask God to fill our empty places.

Demons are exactly opposite in character to Jesus. They enter a person in order to project their own evil nature through that person. So what we are after is to cast out demons and their influence in order to replace them with Jesus and the fruit of the Spirit.

Chapter 3 - Are You Set Free?

Therefore in order to get free, the house must be filled and kept filled. Otherwise evil spirits will return and may return in greater force than before. What is the purpose of the baptism in the Holy Ghost? Power!

The power of the Holy Ghost is manifested through the gifts of the Spirit in 1Corinthians 12:7-11. The entire book of Acts shows how the power of the Holy Ghost operates through these gifts of the Spirit. Demons despise these gifts of the Holy Spirit and cause men to despise them, too. Why? Because demons know that the operation of these supernatural gifts of power counters their work. When the devil has you angry and feeling that your self-worth is beneath everybody else's, then he (the devil) has created Spiritual Bondage.

Bondage - Physical slavery or a reference to life prior to knowing Jesus Christ. (Romans 8:15, Galatians 4:7- 9)

*Opposite words of bondage are: liberation, emancipation, liberty and freedom.

It's because the devil makes you think about nothing but the things of the flesh, such as fast women, drugs, money, etc., until the flesh controls your will. Consequently, you do nothing but those things and they destroy your love for life by making life hard with heavy burdens. The first thing you need to know is why you are in bondage in the first place. Do the women (men), drugs, money or even alcohol have you in bondage or is there something else? In the beginning stage of this group, you will learn what is behind bondage. Take a moment to think about the following questions:

1.) Do you feel sick, or trapped in bondage?
2.) Is my problem a disease that lies in my body, or do I have to put forth an effort to keep my problems? In other words, is there a certain behavior that accompanies my bondage state?
3.) Is my state of bondage like other diseases that does not make me think, or is it trying to control my mind.

If you feel trapped and are putting forth effort to stay in the state you're in, and cannot keep your problems out of your mind, then you are in bondage and are not free. Bondage is not a disease that we caught and need medicine to cure; it is a spirit that we live with, which must be broken spiritually. 'Miracles are nothing

Chapter 3 - Are You Set Free?

other than God's ordinary truth seen with surprised eyes.'

Numbers 14:35

"I the Lord have said, I will surely do it unto all this evil congregation, that are gathered together against me: in this wilderness they shall be consumed, and there they shall die."

The physical part of bondage is the unstoppable use of something that is out of the will of God. The spiritual part of bondage is the overpowering thoughts and desires to do a thing. However, what leads us into bondage in the first place is a lack of understanding that we cannot make it in this life without God. If we cannot control our minds, then how can we control our lives? Our destiny, our peace, our joy, our strength, meaning and purpose is in a right relationship with God.

We are responsible for our own spiritual life because by our own choices (free will), we open the door to this overpowering force. Likewise, we are responsible for our deliverance for by our own choice we must turn to God and ask for His help. As much as you want to

Free the Trapped Soul

live right in your own power you cannot; all men face this problem.

You cannot live right (righteous) without God. You need His help and power to do so. Therefore, God sent Jesus His Son to give us the power by destroying sin in our flesh. If you stay with God, you will be okay, but if you walk away living life based on your own terms, you will fail.

Chapter 4

Why God?

John 4:23-24

"But the hour cometh, and now is, when the true worshippers shall worship the Father in spirit and in truth: for the Father seeketh such to worship him."

Why God?

I used to ask myself that question, but it is clear, 'why God.' He sustained me in all my troubles, hell and abusive life. He kept me when I was getting beat by broom sticks and protected me in a house fire. That's 'why God!' Because we cannot get free from bondage, living life in a pigpen and, or spiritual emptiness any other way! All bondage, living life in a pigpen, and spiritual emptiness all arises when the natural superiors fail to rule and natural subordinates fail to obey. A man's body should obey his soul and a man's soul should obey his spirit and when it does not, physical disease results.

Free the Trapped Soul

(3 John 1:2) A man's spirit should obey God (Jesus says I am the Way, Truth and the Life).

Acts of obedience break spiritual bondage!

There's a difference between bondage (strongholds) and temptation.

Bondage
(Bondage makes life hard and bitter).
1.) A force or feeling that unites people.
2.) A binding agreement, especially one that commits someone to make a payment to another.
3.) Join or joined securely to something else.
4.) Establish a relationship based on shared feelings or experiences.

Temptation is not bondage, it is what makes our flesh feel good.

James 1:14

"But every man is tempted, when he is drawn away of his own <u>lust</u> *(when he is thinking about himself), and* <u>enticed</u> *(to attract by offering pleasure)."*

Chapter 4 - Why God?

Temptation is Satan's attempt to get us to think and live outside of God's Word; an attempt to get man to think and act for himself and about himself.

What's the point?

Things that we do not like, never tempt us. Bondage (strongholds) begins with objects that we like. These objects interest us and enchant us to them. The devil knows what you like and dislike; knows what your flesh enjoys. He is the tempter but the only reason he is successful is because he uses what you like. The Samarian woman liked sex with men. Five husbands is a lot of men in a lifetime and number six is not her husband. And you ask yourself, 'Why God?'

There is also times in our life were we feel betrayed, just as the Samarian woman may have felt. I have felt that way when someone I cared for or even a family member 'stabbed me in the back.' My family members talk about me all the time and it's not always in a good way. You know that you are the center of the topic when you walk in the room and everybody stops talking!

Free the Trapped Soul

Matthew 26:21-23

"Now as they were eating, He said, 'Assuredly, I say to you one will betray Me. And they were exceedingly sorrowful, and each of them began to say to Him, Lord is it I? He answered and said, He who dipped his hand with Me in the dish will betray Me.'"

How many of you have had someone sitting right at your dinner table, just as Jesus did, or riding in your car, sleeping in your house sharing the extra room, friends (and please don't forget family members) that have betrayed you and your trust? The feeling is hurtful and it feels like you could die, because of the time, trust and even money you put in the person. You might have even thought, 'How could they do this to me? I know I did!

Can you imagine how Jesus the Christ felt after giving His disciples the authority to heal the sick, give sight to the blind and to raise the lame and dead? "Father, forgive them, because they do not know what they do." (Luke 23:34). You may not be facing persecution now like Jesus was facing, but Christians in other parts of the world are. I'm here to tell you don't

Chapter 4 - Why God?

give up through your betrayal, it will happen. If Christ Jesus could stay on the mission for the remission of sin for the world, and made disciples, and rose on the third day, you, too, will be raised up in Christ Jesus.

Whatever you may be facing or experiencing right now in your life, I encourage you to go through it and see what God will do in your situation. Jesus forgave Judas for his betrayal and we must forgive those who may have betrayed us. Unforgiveness will drain your power in your walk of love in Christ Jesus.

We must let the hurt of the past go. You may be saying to yourself 'I can't forgive that person who betrayed me because you don't know what they did.' Then let me say to you that it doesn't matter what they did! You cannot dwell on the past and things of this world because if you do, no one can see the difference between the world and the Jesus that lives in you.

Even in betrayal we ought to forgive as God forgives us.

Free the Trapped Soul

<u>Galatians 6:7</u>

"We reap what we sow."

When you sow the seeds of forgiveness, love and mercy, than you reap the same harvest. When you set your will to forgive others, God pours out blessing like never before. Unforgiveness stops faith, unforgiveness stops prayers. How many times should I forgive my brother and sisters for their betrayal, lies, cheating and stealing? You may be wondering, 'are you serious about forgiveness?' For the Bible says seventy times seventy. When we hold on to hurt, we hinder God's wonderful work in our lives and prevent His blessing from manifesting. Hanging on to betrayal will make you spiritually empty.

Don't let the demon spirit of betrayal hinder you today from getting to Jesus! It could be your loneliness. It could be your temper or frustration or even your childhood. Whatever it is, get rid of it! Before you know it, God's love, blessings, and power will take complete control over your life.

Chapter 4 - Why God?

You may wonder, just as I had to ask myself 'Why God?'

Chapter 5

Living Among Confusion

It is so confusing when you live life with a lot of conflict. You should understand that we all have had a time when we were confused as hell. I often wonder 'why no one wanted me?' Why I was not with my brothers and sisters. Why my mother hated me so much, and why my father cared for the other woman's children over me (his own flesh and blood)? He still does, today. Our relationship is built around some other woman's grown children. They were shown love, but for me it was 'go to Hell!'

<u>1 Corinthians 14:33</u>

"For God is not a God of disorder but of peace."

Have you realized that wondering and confusion are related? Wondering causes confusion. We live much of our lives and do not realize that the devil has declared war against us, and the mind is where the battle takes place. We need to realize that confusion is a state of being abashed or distracted, perplexed, or a loss of self-possession. We often find ourselves in a confused state when dealing with what is right and what is wrong. Wrong is easy to do! But, if doing what is right makes you think something is wrong then you are operating outside of what God has told you.

You may say, I'm confused, but the devil is a liar. I used to find myself the most confused, or I thought I was confused when I started living for God. You may say, 'how can I a man or woman be confused in God?' I'm not saying that God confused me. What I'm saying is that, I loved what I was doing more than life itself. After making God the center of my life, I know whenever I do something wrong. How? Because the Holy Spirit convicts me, so I no longer wonder in confusion.

To this day, I know God had a plan for my life just as He has a plan for yours. Being confused is a trick of the devil and in doing so we lack knowledge that God has given us.

Chapter 5 - Living Among Confusion

Let's explore the Scriptures to help us understand how to overcome wondering and confusion and to receive what is needed from God.

<u>James 1:5-8</u>

"If any of you lack wisdom, let him ask of God, who gives to all liberally and without reproach, and it will be given to him. But let him ask in faith, with no doubting, for he who doubts is like a wave of the sea driven and tossed by the wind. For let no man suppose that he will receive anything from the Lord; he is a double-minded man, unstable in all his ways."

By wisdom, James is talking not only about knowledge but also the ability to make wise decisions in difficult circumstances. Whenever we need wisdom, we can pray to God and he will generously supply what we need. Christians don't have to grope around in the dark, hoping to stumble upon answers. We can ask for God's wisdom to guide our choices.

Wisdom means "discernment," which begins with respect for God that leads to right living and results in increased ability to tell right from wrong. God is willing to give us wisdom, but we will be unable to receive it if our goals are self-centered instead of God-centered. To learn God's Will, we need to read His Word and ask Him to show us how to obey it. Then we must do what He tells us. We must not only believe in the existence of God but also in His loving care.

This includes relying on God and expecting that He will hear and answer when we pray. We must put away our critical attitudes when we come to Him. God does not grant every thoughtless or selfish request. We must have confidence that God will align our desires with His purpose. A doubtful mind is not completely convinced that God's ways are best. It treats God's Word like any human advice and retains the option to disobey. It vacillates between allegiance, subjective feelings, the world's ideas, and God's commands. If your faith is new, weak or struggling remember that you can trust God. Then be loyal to Him to stabilize your wavering or doubtful mind, and commit yourself wholeheartedly to God.

If you have ever seen the constant rolling of huge waves at sea, you know how restless they are subject to the forces of nature. Doubt leaves a person as unsettled as the restless waves. If you want to stop being tossed

Chapter 5 - Living Among Confusion

about, rely on God to show you what is best for you. Ask Him for wisdom and trust that He will give it to you. If you are a very curious, inquisitive person (or should I say just nosey), you have to know and figure everything out in order to be satisfied. You need to seek God and pray that He will show you that the constant reasoning is the basis for your confusion, and that it may be preventing you from receiving what God wants to give you. You must put aside carnal reasoning if you ever expect to have true discernment.

Proverbs 3:5

"Lean on, trust in, and be confident in the Lord with all your heart and mind and do not rely on your own insight or understanding."

In other words, do not rely on reasoning. Reasoning opens the door for deception and brings about much confusion. Beware that when the mind is filled with doubt, it is not normal; at least not for the Christian who intends to be victorious. The believer who intends to win the war remembers that it is fought in the mind.

Free the Trapped Soul

In order to get out of a state of confusion we must lose the attachments. The moment we become attached to a substance, behaviors, object or people we lose our freedom and become confused. You were born free; we lose our freedom when we become attached to things. It is easy to be brought into confusion, first you fight with will-power not to become attached. You must NOT give up. As long as you fighting, the devil cannot handcuff you; it is when you stop fighting that he can handcuff you.

Confusion is a state where a person is internally forced to give energy to things. A preoccupation enslaves a person's will and desires. How we become free from confusion and attachments is through detaching and repentance. In the next chapter we will see how to detach and have a true repentance.

Chapter 6

Detachment through True Repentance

Before we can talk about detachments, we must first find out what we are attached to. I got attached to all the wrong things in life, drugs, women, stealing, robbery... you name it I did it. Just to fit in with people who really didn't have a care in the world for me; they didn't care if I lived or died. Attachments are created not by things that do not make you feel good, but by things that DO make you feel good. The attachment to a behavior, object or person is connected to the pleasure one gets out of those things.

The attachment is the desire the flesh has for an emotion, pleasure, feeling or thought. People fall in love then depend on the sensation that they get from the object of their desire to give them a particular feeling or experience, and become attached to it.

Free the Trapped Soul

In truth attachment is a counterfeit and deceptive spiritual experience that has only a temporary result, which is why you must not keep chasing after your attachments. Attachments are the feeling one gets from the object, person or thing that is why it is so hard to break free. It is because your flesh loves it so, even when the feeling never lasts long. Now one must become detached from these spiritual attachments.

Isaiah 10:27

"And it shall come to pass in the day, that his burden shall be taken away from off thy shoulder, and his yoke from off thy neck, and the yoke shall be destroyed because of the anointing."

Detachment is the word used in spiritual traditions to describe freedom of desire, not freedom from desire. God will never take away desire, but He will break attachments of desire because we were not meant to be made slaves by our desires. The anointing is the power of the Holy Spirit to break the attachments of desire that keeps you from having a free will. God breaks the attachments of desire because these are prisons and the strongholds of attachment make us spiritual prisoners.

Chapter 6 - Detachment through True Repentance

God created man to have free will that is His purpose for our lives. Free will gives us the chance to choose God. That is the only reason He frees us. God will never allow man to stay in bondage to the point that he cannot choose Him. We cannot rid ourselves of attachments through our own efforts, but we can freely turn to God or turn away from God. Therefore, instead of leaving us to live a dry and uncaring life with little hope and meaning, God breaks the yoke, liberates our desires and renews our passion for life.

Repentance - "to Change the Mind": the spiritual change implied in a sinner's return to God. The term signifies to have another mind, to change the opinion or purpose with regard to lifestyle.

When the woman of Samaria left her water pot and went her way, it signified a change of mind. The water pot represented her way of life. If you are not ready to leave your way of life behind you will stay in bondage, and God cannot operate in your mess. Man can only move forward in life from where he is to the place he should be. The Samarian woman decided to change her life by turning to the True God. The waterpot represented the heavy burden she was carrying because of the things she did. The false gods of our strongholds will cause us to live a life of shame and guilt because of things we did, also.

Matthew 11:28-30

"Come unto me, all ye that labour and are heavy laden, and I will give you rest. Take my yoke upon you, and learn of me; for I am meek and lowly in heart: and ye shall find rest unto your souls. For my yoke is easy, and my burden is light."

We must know how to plant beliefs in our spirit man.

Genesis 8:22

"While the earth remained, seedtime and harvest, and cold and heat, and summer and winter, and day and night shall not cease."

There are only two types of words, there is truth (the Word of God) and there are lies, (words from Satan).

Chapter 6 - Detachment through True Repentance

John 8:44

"Ye are of your father the devil, and the lust of your father ye will do. He was a murderer from the beginning, and abode not in the truth, because there is no truth in him. When he speaketh a lie, he speaketh of his own: for he is a liar, and the father of it."

God and Satan are both in the business of planting thoughts and words. What makes God and Satan different is that Satan's word steals, kills, and destroys life, but God's Word heals, delivers and sets free. Sow a thought you reap an action, sow an action you reap a habit, sow a habit you reap a character, sow a character you reap a destiny. Our future is determined by the thoughts and words that we sow.

Let's define sow:
1.) To scatter (seed) over the ground for growing.
2.) To impregnate (a growing medium) with seed.

This is what Satan does, he scatters thought seeds in the world to impregnate as many as he can with deceptive ideas that produce destruction in our lives. Thoughts planted in our minds produce actions. Nothing begins in our lives without a thought. The very reason why you are here in this group is because of a thought. The problem has been that Satan has had our attention which enabled him to plant thoughts into our lives.

Ephesians 6:12

"For we wrestle not against flesh and blood, but against principalities, against powers, against the ruler of the darkness of this world, against spiritual wickedness in high places."

If you don't confront your own issues and your own capacity for sin, you remain a well-marked target for the devil. If you don't admit that you are vulnerable to committing sin in a certain area, you remain vulnerable in that area. So how can God plant any belief when you are allowing Satan to plant beliefs? Why? Because in being so sure that you'll never commit the sin in question, you take no safeguards against it. And without safeguards, you are wide open to the devil's attack and he will sow beliefs like anger, hostile attitudes, fear, and weakness. But I'm telling you, there's a problem behind your problem, and that real problem is the belief of a sinful nature. If you have never asked God to forgive you of your sins and change your sinful

Chapter 6 - Detachment through True Repentance

nature, do it right now. God stands ready to forgive you and to begin planting beliefs that will grow into beautiful fruit of the Spirit.

Psalm 126:5

"They that sow in tears shall reap in Joy."

Galatians 6:7

"Be not deceived; God is not mocked: for whatsoever a man soweth, that shall he also reap."

A thought sown in the mind creates actions or lifestyles and actions sown create habits.

Habit - A recurrent often unconscious pattern of behavior that is acquired through frequent repetition; also, an established disposition or place of the mind or character. It is a tiresome course of action.

In other words a habit is rooted in the thoughts that are planted in the mind; it is not in the body. A habit is simply something that we have become accustomed to doing. It is a pattern, a particular lifestyle. And the only way to get out of a habit is to desire another lifestyle. And that won't happen if you are still thinking that same way about things that have become the object of your life. That is why bad experiences with things in life are important, because they force you to start thinking another way about life.

Are you tired of the lifestyle you are living? How do you really feel about the way you have been living? What are you sowing? Now here is where real danger begins, because habits force us to live a certain way.

Character is not personality, it has nothing to do with whether or not you are a funny person, or argumentative, or eccentric. Character goes hand in hand with one's ethics. Ethics is a matter of personal character, of what kind of person you are inside, and it is not merely a matter of whether you follow rules (even though it is our ethical duty to do so).

2 Corinthians 5:17

"Therefore if any man be in Christ, he is a new creature: old things are passed away; behold, all things are become new."

Chapter 6 - Detachment through True Repentance

You now have the inner ability to choose to be morally good, in sum when it comes to the kind of person you are, you and you alone ultimately determines your own destiny.

1.} The unexamined life is not worth living.
2.} The greatest fault is to be conscious of none.
3.} Character is what we do in the dark when no one is looking.
4.} Character is higher than intellect, what is the point of knowing good if you don't keep trying to become a good person?

Jeremiah 29:11

"For I know the thoughts that I think towards you, saith the Lord, thoughts of peace, and not of evil, to give you an expected end."

Whatever one reflects into his or her mind and dwell on tends to take form. In other words thoughts planted in our minds grow to real conditions.

Chapter 7

Falling in Love with Lies

It is true that every person at one point and time in their life gives up on the idea of a high quality of life and lives at a very low standard. I started believing in my own lies that drugs and money gets the girls. I had this false insight that it was all good and that it would take me places. Yes, it did and I thank God that I never had a STD, but the places and where it took me was a mess. And all the mistakes I made I blamed on everybody else for my lies.

I would lie even when I didn't have to when the truth was easy, but the truth wasn't in me. Therefore falling in love with lies is a form of quitting. Why has the person given up? One reason so many people give up is that they believe that we can only survive with the support of a little white lie. Therefore living without the ability to exercise the truth is living life in the tombs.

Free the Trapped Soul

There is a belief that the daily hardship and suffering people face can only be endured. That it is acceptable by wherever and however we find a way to feel good, so we look for ways to escape and fall in love with lies. We fall into temptation by selfish desires. Temptation looks goods to us. Next we believe a lie about the thing that tempts us. Then we become hooked when we take the bait. There are things that we must know about belief.

Proverbs 23:7

"For as a man thinks in his heart, so is he."

1.} Belief is the law of our lives.
2.} Belief determines what we experience.
3.} Belief can put you under the power of a thing.
4.} What put us under the power of our strongholds was something we believed.
5.} Many believe the lie that they are in bondage and the lie keeps us hooked.

Chapter 7 - Falling in Love with Lies

<u>Mark 5:5</u>

"And always, night and day, he was in the mountains, and in the tombs, crying, and cutting himself with stones."

The fact is we're killing ourselves. Countless men are living in lies. You can kill a person with your words, your attitude, and your absence. How many people are suicidal or messed up in their minds because of the lies you told?

The Bible is God's thoughts about the way man is supposed to live. It is the truth. The Bible is not a book it is the Word of God. There is a law in our world that states that the one who invents the thing determines how it should function. God is the creator of man and life and He says in Luke 4:4, "And Jesus answered him, saying, it is written. That man shall not live by bread alone, but by every word of God."

If a mechanic says put gas in the tank of your car and we put water into it the car breaks down. It is the same with our thoughts, if God (Who is our mechanic) says that man must function by the Word and we believe other words and thoughts about life and ourselves… We will malfunction, in other words we will break down to the lies of man. I know this to be true because I used to live with lies. I was the liar.

The devil knows that if he can get us to accept words about ourselves outside of God's Word, then he can win a great victory over our life. That is why the Bible tells us that Satan is the great deceiver. Man's enemy is the devil.

Revelation 12:9

"And the great dragon was cast out, that old serpent, called the Devil, and Satan which deceiveth the whole world; he was cast out into the earth, and his angels were cast out with him."

By now, you can see the real power of the lies of the enemy. Lies are the devil's greatest weapon. The degree of control to which he exercises lies over us is proportional to the lies we believe. The more lies we believe, the more the enemy will control, enslave and destroy us. The lies can come from everywhere: the attitude and beliefs of society, co-workers, friends, parents, and even our own minds. Satan uses them all to

Chapter 7 - Falling in Love with Lies

try to defeat us. The solution is to know the truth about God and ourselves that are found in the scriptures.

Sometimes Christians know that the source of true freedom is in the Word of God, but cannot apply it because of sin of parents or others or even some horrible experience that leaves a lasting wound. 'Sticks and stones may break my bones, but names will never hurt me' is a lie straight from the pit of Hell. Words can hurt your life; there is power in words. But there is more Power in the Word!

Let's take a moment to look at Samson, and how Satan used words to destroy him…

Samson was called by God to become a judge (prophet) for the people of God (Israel). The God of Abraham, Isaac and Jacob anointed him with supernatural strength which led to his ability to conquer the Philistine army and liberate Israel from their oppression.

Although he had several public victories he had quite a few personal failures. One of the greatest of failures of Samson was not a massive army but the strength of an ungodly woman's influence which targeted his sinful passion. This same man who defeated a thousand enemy soldiers with the jawbone of a donkey is the same man who told the secret of his strength to a seductive woman named Delilah. The biblical account reveals that Samson's strength was due to the uncut locks of hair upon his head. And when he told Delilah this secret, she put a razor to his hair while he slept. Upon awakening from sleep, he had no more supernatural strength and was ultimately captured by the Philistines and they gauged out his eyes and imprisoned him in a dungeon. This happened because of the power of Delilah's words.

There are lessons to learn from Samson:

First, there are two realms of life:
1] Physical, which is motivated or influenced by desires.
2] Spiritual, which is motivated or influenced by words.

    Delilah knew the harvest she wanted out of her dealings with Samson, so she just kept sowing the thought through her seductive ways to appease his lustful desires. Delilah represented Satan: Deceiver who pretended to love, a liar and a destroyer.

Chapter 7 - Falling in Love with Lies

Second, four things resulted from deception:
1] Loss of self-respect
2] Spiritual blindness
3] Bondage
4] Destruction

In any group of men, I know in my heart that every kind of problem is present, every kind of need, every kind of weakness, every kind of struggle is created through the power in a spoken word. I also know that today is the time when we need to confront those problems, needs, weaknesses, and struggles with the Word of God. It's time that we begin to challenge and confront ourselves about what we hold within ourselves, because there's power in the Word of God.

When a man ignores the commandments of God and refuses to turn to God and acknowledge Him as Lord, the worst punishment God gives to that man on this earth is to turn him over to himself, to give him over to his own reprobate mind. And they lose the power in the spoken word. Can you be real and truthful with yourself and realize that you believe thoughts that are hurting your life? This is the place where healing begins

Free the Trapped Soul

to take effort in your life. I have discovered that it is even hard for me to be truthful when looking within myself. I have nothing else to believe now. This world has no definition for me. Truth and error cannot co-exist, so they will fight against each other like lions in a pit.

Chapter 8

Being Raised from the Dead

<u>Mark 16:6</u>

"But he said to them, do not be alarmed, you seek Jesus of Nazareth, who was crucified. He is risen! He is not here. See the place where they laid Him."

Was I raised from the dead? The answer would be 'yes.' Not from a fleshly death but from a spiritual death. I was dead to a good life and to all those who finally loved me. Yes, God called onto my spirit man and I was raised from the dead. I was walking around like a lot of you, just too stubborn to lay down and have dirt thrown over me.

The resurrection is vitally important for many reasons: Jesus first kept His promise to rise from the dead, so we can believe He will keep all of His promises. The resurrection also ensures that the ruler of God's eternal Kingdom will be the Living Christ, not just an idea, hope or dream. Christ's resurrection gives us assurance that we will be resurrected. The power of God that brought Christ's body back from the dead is available to us to bring our morally and spiritually dead selves back to life, so that we can change and grow. The resurrection provides substance of the Church's witness to the world. We do not merely tell lessons from the life of a good teacher we proclaim the reality of the resurrection of Jesus, the Christ.

The reason some of us are walking around spiritually dead is because we carry on the curses, or should I say, strongholds, of our grandparents, parents, and even some that we put upon ourselves.

These curses are passed down from preceding generations through belief systems, ways of thinking and tolerated behaviors, etc. Thoughts from our forefathers are impressed and planted in our minds and grow to real conditions as they leach themselves onto our psyche. This is the problem of people walking around dead, and is ultimately a spiritual problem. Spirituality is the essence of human existence. We are not material beings on a spiritual journey; but spiritual beings who need an earthly journey to become fully spiritual. Spirituality is

Chapter 8 - Being Raised from the Dead

about growth and expansion, newness and creativity. Spirituality is about being, and being is about why there is something, rather than nothing. To be truly human is to have an inner self; a life from within full of God's power. We reason and make decisions using our minds and our hearts. According to Proverbs 23:7, "for as he thinks in his heart, so he is. "

We live what we truly believe. How we act does not always reflect what we say, but it does reflect our belief system. If your life is immoral, dishonest, proud, or depraved it is a sure sign that your belief system is immoral, dishonest, proud and depraved. We must always be encouraged.

Job 6:11

"What strength do I have, that I should hope? And what is my end, that I should prolong my life."

I, too, felt like the Israelites in the wilderness, not having a positive vision for my life and no dreams. I knew where I came from, but not where I was going. Everything I was thinking about was based on my past. We often as children from broken homes always hear "you are just like your daddy." Then you look at your daddy and see that he's really not what you expect from a father: no hugs, reasoning and no love. But I'm going to tell you the good news. Be encouraged!

Let's take a look at the book of Job, as we know the story of Job. He lost all he had through no fault of his own. As he struggled to understand why all these things were happening to him, it became clear that he was not meant to know the reasoning. He would have to face life with the answer and explanations held back. Only then would his faith fully develop and he was encouraged.

We must experience life as Job did: one day at a time without complete answers to all of life's questions. Will we be like Job and trust God no matter what happens? Will we stay encouraged, or will we give into the temptation of the devil to say that God doesn't care? When God does a work in your life, He does it in calmness. He brings about a peace in your life. All hell may be breaking out against you and around you, but you can sit back and be encouraged that God and all His awesome mercies will bring you through. As we see calamity and suffering in the Book of Job, we must

Chapter 8 - Being Raised from the Dead

remember that we live in a fallen world where good behavior is not always rewarded and bad behavior is not always punished.

Fathers, Mothers, Brothers, and Sisters, be of good encouragement to yourselves, children and family members as Job showed deep concern for the spiritual welfare of his children. Fearful that they have sinned unknowingly, he offered sacrifices for them unto God. Parents, today, can we show the same concern by praying for your children. Give a sacrifice of praise. This means sacrificing some time each day to ask God to forgive them, to help them grow in the Lord, to protect them and to help them to please the Lord Jesus Christ.

Satan tries to do any and everything in his power to discourage you, and to make you corrupt through your own pride. God's people can overcome the devil's attack through the power of God by knowing that Satan will do anything to gain a soul. Knowing this we should remain close to the one who is greater and that's God Himself.

Chapter 9

Lacking Faith and the Power Thereof!

<u>Romans 10:17</u>

"So then faith cometh by hearing, and hearing by the word of God."

We often face situations where we want to throw in the towel, and just give up on life, relationships, family and church. Why? Because we lack in the faith we need to go on. I had no faith in myself or anybody else. Faith was something of the far future, but it was not for me. Would God save me, would God hear my cries?

Let me give you an example about the time I received my call into ministry. It was one of those days when I was coming down from a high (a fleshly high). I already knew the Voice of God and knew what He could do in my life, if I let Him. I tried to run several times because I didn't understand the mysteries. I was lying in my basement and God started to minister to me by means of television, using two great mighty men of God. Both men ministered to my soul, and I started to cry. It's not that I had no faith; it was that Satan was trying to destroy me and my faith with lies.

Matthew 17:20

"And Jesus said unto them because of your unbelief: for verily I say unto you, if ye have faith as a grain of a mustard seed, ye shall say unto this mountain, remove hence to yonder place; and it shall remove; and nothing shall be impossible unto you."

In Matthew 17:20, Jesus wasn't condemning the disciples for substandard faith. He was trying to show them the importance faith has and how it would be used in their future ministry. If you are facing a problem that seems as big and immovable as a mountain look to Christ Jesus for more faith! Only then will you be able to overcome the obstacles that may stand in your way. You see when God tells us something or asks us to do something; the faith to believe it or to do it comes with the Word from God. Faith brings about power and Satan knows how dangerous we will be with a heart full

Chapter 9 - Lacking Faith and the Power Thereof!

of faith. And without faith we end up living life in a pig pen, like the prodigal son. Lack of knowledge concerning God's Will and purpose for our lives leads us to a life of self-centeredness.

Hosea 4:6

"My people are destroyed for lack of knowledge: because thou hast rejected knowledge, I will also reject thee, that thou shalt be no priest to me; seeing thou hast forgotten the law of thy God, I will also forget thy children."

God has a plan and a way for us to live our life, which is called the Word of God. Most of us grew up not knowing or understanding the purpose of Scripture and therefore a lack of knowledge that leads us to live life on our own terms. Like the prodigal son, we decided to live life our way, on our terms, taking our destiny into our own hands. Self-centeredness is about my way, God-centeredness understands that God created you and has a purpose and plan for your life. Self-centeredness - a lot of mistakes and failures are experienced in our lives, because of the choices we make that are outside of God's Will.

Free the Trapped Soul

The life of the prodigal son became one big party, which amounted to years of wasted time in his life. When we lack understanding as to whom we are and the reason we are here on earth, life becomes a waste. Anything that operates out of its purpose is not productive. It is malfunctioning. A train does not know it is a train after being on the track and thinks it's a boat; then we look like a fool thinking we're a boat after being on a track.

We begin to think of ourselves as worthless and failures. Naturally, if we are not functioning as we were built to function, we begin to think that something is wrong with us… This is the deception of the enemy (Satan); this is what he is after. Satan is after our self-worth when we finally, totally accept the idea that we are a failure, worthless or flawed. The will to keep trying is broken and we lose hope and give up on our dreams. The prodigal son began his journey with a plan. The problem that he was having is that it was not God's plan for his life. His plan had failed and then he had lost all hope and his spirit was broken. His will had surrendered to an idea that he was a failure when the truth was that only his *plan* was a failure.

Chapter 9 - Lacking Faith and the Power Thereof!

At this point, his life is spiritually bankrupt and he is experiencing a deep inner shame. To fill the void he looked to something to replace the emptiness. The Bible says that he began to be in want. In other words, the natural reaction to spiritual bankruptcy is to find something to fill the void. Let's look at what happened next, the prodigal son joined himself to the citizens of that country. In other words, he became attached to some things other than God. This is when bondage occurs in our lives, bondage is joining one's self to sex, drugs, alcohol and even people. These are the first things we try to fill the void with. Yes, it feels good spiritually and emotionally (so we think) and if just for a moment, the object of our attachment takes us away from our inner pain. Because our problems have not gone away, naturally, we need more of that object that makes us feel good to deal with them. For instance, I go deeper and deeper in my mess. The only problem is me, which make me more ashamed; I do things that I would have never done before, therefore life becomes increasingly empty.

At this point in our lives, we should come to ourselves and realize that the life we chose outside of the Will of the Father has become a mess. We are responsible to choose to walk out of bondage. While in bondage it can become a lifestyle. God has chosen the right way for man to live. We must recognize to repent of the life we chose and return to the Father. We are either living life on our terms and are heading for the pigpen, or we have decided to follow God's way and be blessed. It is not meant for man to lack in anything that God has meant for us to have, but when we go out we must go out with a Word from God.

Mark 16:15

"And then he told them, go into all the world and preach the good news to everyone, everywhere."

Jesus told his disciples to go into all parts of the world, telling everyone that he had paid the penalty for sin and that those who believed in Him can and shall be forgiven and live eternally with the Father. Christians, today, in all parts of the world are telling this good news to people who haven't heard about Christ. The driving force that carries missionaries around the world and sets Christ's Church in motion is the faith that comes from His resurrection.

Chapter 9 - Lacking Faith and the Power Thereof!

Who are you telling about what God has done for you? We woke up this morning able to walk, talk, breathe and see. We should be giving God some praise and telling somebody. The hell we put ourselves through and God was right there to pull us up and out. Go tell somebody! I'm just glad that I can tell my story to the addict, the homeless, and people in jail cells and those who feel lost in a sense. Why? Because I was there, but praise be to God, I can tell somebody how I got over. My soul looks back and wonders how I got over.

Do you ever feel as though you don't have the skills or determination to be a witness for Christ? You must personally realize that Jesus rose from the dead and lives in you today. As you grow in your relationship with Christ, He will give you both the opportunities and the inner strength to tell His message.

<u>Matthew 4:18-20</u>

"And Jesus, walking by the sea of Galilee, saw two brethren, Simon called Peter, and Andrew his brother casting a net into the

sea; for they were fishers. And he saith unto them, follow me, and I will make you fishers of men. And they straightway left their nets, and followed him."

Jesus told Peter and Andrew to leave their fishing business and begin fishing for people, helping others to find God. Jesus was calling them away from their productive trade to be productive, spiritually. We all need to fish for souls. If we practice Christ's teaching and share the good news with others, we will be able to draw those around us unto Christ like fishermen who pulls fish into his boat with nets. Be a witness for Christ Jesus.

Isaiah 43:10

"Ye are my witness, saith the Lord, and my servant whom I have chosen: that ye may know and believe me, and understand that I am he; before me there was no God formed, neither shall there be after me."

Israel's task was to be a witness telling the world Who God is and what He had done. Believers today share the same responsibility of being God's witnesses. Do people know what God is like through your word

Chapter 9 - Lacking Faith and the Power Thereof!

and example? They cannot see God directly, but they can see Him reflected in you. Don't be of little faith, ending up in a pig pen, but go tell somebody about the goodness of the Lord.

Chapter 10 –

Reaping the Benefits

<u>Matthew 5:5</u>

"Blessed are the meek: for they shall inherit the earth."

I hurt so many nights, I cried so many hours, but I received my reward when I received God in my life. My life got better; God even gave me a good second wife (a woman of God's own heart) and a stable life. What a reward!

Jesus began His sermon with words that seemed to contradict other's opinions. But God's way of living usually contradicts the world's way of living. If you want to live for God, you must be ready to say and do what seems strange to the world. You must be willing to give when others take, to love when others hate, to help when others abuse. By giving up your own rights in order to serve others, you will one day receive everything God has in store for you.

Matthew 5:12

"Rejoice, and be exceeding glad: for great is your reward in heaven: for they persecuted the prophets which were before you."

Jesus said to rejoice when we're persecuted for our faith. Persecution can be good because, it takes our eyes off earthly rewards, it strips away superficial beliefs, it strengthens the faith of those who endure, our attitude through it serves as an example to others to follow.

We can be comforted knowing that God's greatest prophets were persecuted (Elijah, Jeremiah, Daniel), and the fact that we are being faithful. Faithless people would be unnoticed. In the future God will reward the faithful by receiving them into His eternal Kingdom where there is no more persecution.

2 Timothy 4:14

"Alexander the coppersmith did me much evil: the Lord reward him according to his works."

Chapter 10 - Reaping the Benefits

Alexander witnessed against Paul at his trial, just as people will witness against you, but keep in mind that God will give them their reward, according to their works. If they hate or do evil, I pity their reward from God. I pray that you not do evil for evil and dirt for dirt, instead, let God fight your battles.

1 Corinthians 3:8

"Now he that planteth and he that waterth are one: and every man shall receive his own reward according to his labour."

Labor for the way of the Lord, that your labor will not be in vain. God has promised us great things and He is not a man that, can or will lie, to us for we are His children. And I know that God has promised me a reward in Him for living right; I will have my joy.

Nehemiah 8:10

"Then he said unto them, go your way, eat the fat, and drink the sweet, and send potions unto them for whom nothing is prepared; for this day is holy unto the Lord; neither be ye sorry; for the joy of the Lord is your strength."

The people wept openly when they heard God's laws and realized how far they were from obeying them. But Ezra told them they should be filled with joy, because the day was sacred. It was time to celebrate and give gifts to those in need. Celebrate is not to be self-centered.

Ezra connected celebration with giving. This gave those in need an opportunity to celebrate as well. Often we celebrate and give to others even when we don't feel like it; we are strengthened spiritually and filled with joy. Enter into celebration that honors God and allows Him to fill you with His joy. We must not look at others and ignore their pain, but make a joyful noise unto the Lord for everything He has done.

Psalm 126:5

"They that sow in tears shall reap in joy."

God's ability to restore life is beyond our understanding. Forests are burned down and are able to grow back; bones are broken and mend as they are healed. Even grief is not a permanent condition. Our tears can be seeds that will grow into harvest of joy

Chapter 10 - Reaping the Benefits

because God is able to bring something good out of a tragedy. When burdened by sorrow, know that your times of grief will end then you will again find joy. We must be patient as we wait because God's great harvest of joy is coming!

John 16:24

"Hitherto have ye asked nothing in my name; ask, and ye shall receive, that your joy may be full."

Jesus is telling and instructing us to just ask and it shall be given unto us.

James 1:2-4

"My brethren, count it all joy when ye fall into divers temptations; knowing this, that the trying of your faith worketh patience. But let patience have her perfect work, that ye may be perfect and entire, wanting nothing."

James doesn't say *'if* trouble comes' your way, but *whenever* it does. He assumes that we will have trouble and that it is possible to profit from it. The point is not to pretend to be happy when we face pain but to have a positive outlook. Let it be an opportunity for joy, because of what troubles can produce in your life.

James tells us to turn our hardship into times of learning. Tough times can teach us perseverance. We can't really know the depth of our character until we see how we react under pressure. It is easy to be kind to others when everything is going well, but can we still be kind when others are treating us unfairly?

God wants to make us mature and complete, not keeping us from pain. Instead of complaining about struggles, we should see them as opportunities for growth. Thank God for promising to be with you in rough times. Ask Him to help you to solve your problems, or give you the strength to endure them, then be patient. God will not leave you alone with your problems; He will stay close and help you grow, and bring you joy.

Chapter 11

Thank God for His Grace and Mercy

<u>Hebrews 12:2</u>

"Looking unto Jesus the author and finisher of our faith; who for the joy that was set before him endured the cross, despising the shame, and is set down at the right hand of the house of God."

Remember when we were living outside of God's Will. I had you where it all began in the Garden of Eden. Think about when Adam and Eve sinned against God and as a result of their actions they experienced a life of shame. The good news is where shame began it also ended with Jesus Christ on the cross. When Christ died on the cross He took away all our sins and with it our guilt and shame, and today those who accept His grace are free, from guilt, sin and shame.

Grace is a spiritual experience. Grace stands for gift; it is the gift of being accepted before we become acceptable. You must accept a gift.

Romans 5:15

"But not as the offence, so also is the free gift. For if through the offence of one many be dead, much more the grace of God, and the gift by grace, which is by one man, Jesus Christ, hath abounded unto many."

Most people who experience the grace of God, experience it on one or more of four levels. We experience grace as pardon; we are forgiven for wrongs we have done. Pardoning grace is the answer to guilt. We experience grace as acceptance; we are reunited with God and our true selves, accepted, cradled, held, affirmed, and loved. Accepting grace is the answer to shame. We experience grace as power; it provides a spiritual energy to shed the heaviness of shame and in lightness of grace, move us towards the true self God means for us to be. We experience grace as gratitude; it gives us a sense of appreciation for the gift of life, a sense of wonder and sometimes elation at the lavish generosity of God. One may ask, 'how do we receive grace? We

Chapter 11 Thank God for His Grace and Mercy

receive it by Confession, Forgiveness, Repentance and Love.

Nothing portrays our vulnerability to grace more profoundly than the imagery of the desert and the garden. Eden represents the garden that is our birthplace and our destiny, our home and our promised land. Humanity struggles with a lot of things but my struggle was addiction, it was a journey through the wilderness of idolatry, temptations, trials and loss. But there in my wilderness, God's grace was always available to guide, protect, empower and transform me, and His grace is there for you, too.

The most powerful scriptural metaphor for our journey is the desert sojourn of the Hebrews. God led the people of Israel out of slavery towards the Promised Land, but their journey took them through great loss. In the desert they expressed all the characteristics of a trapped soul, an addict, a whore, a beggar, and every other ungodly thing. Their personality to a degree was so agonizing for God and as frustrating for Moses as it was for themselves. We, too, are so fed up with our life that we want to throw in the towel, like the Israelites. They experienced the stress and fear of withdrawal symptoms, longing for the old days of slavery. We may not long for slavery but if our souls are trapped then we to become slaves. We begin to hoard more stuff than we need. We deceive ourselves with idolatry and excuses. We make resolutions to obey God's commandments, only to apostatize when left to ourselves. We get so caught up in ourselves that our souls are kidnapped to a degree that they become lost and are surrounded by the enemies. We act in self-centered ways, concerned for only one-self, in manipulative ways with self-images so eroded that at times we wish we had died, just as the Israelites wish they had died in slavery. Yet through it all, God's grace and mercy was upon you and I. He protected us, suffered over us, commanded things to happen for us, and today is continually inviting and empowering us to choose, to trust and to love Him and others.

The desert is where the battle with attachments takes place. Your desert may be in your very own homes or upon the streets you hang. The saga of the desert tells of a journey out of slavery, through the desert, towards the garden that is home. But it is much more than a journey; it is the discovery of the depths of weakness, the power of grace and the price of both. Moreover, what takes place in your desert is not simply difficult

Chapter 11 Thank God for His Grace and Mercy

travel and adventurous learning, but it is repentance and conversion, the transformation mixed motivations into purified desire, the greening of the desert into garden through the Living Water of grace. There is no geographic journey here; it all takes place within our hearts. And what happens is not only freedom from sin and purification, but also a loving courtship, a homemaking between the human soul and its Creator.

Do I believe in grace? My answer would be 'yes,' God has extended His grace to me on several occasions. I look back over my life and see, and hear, and feel the gun lodged in my head. Because I was so high I thought it was a joke that this was happening to me! I was a mild-mannered person but I had done some people wrong, and they wanted me dead. But the grace of God jammed the gun and I walked away untouched! I'm not saying I was all that, *but God*. I thank God for that extended grace and mercy in my life. God has given me grace through my drug addiction, my prison terms, and through my childhood. Can you reflect on how much grace God has given *to you*? I know when I look back I just begin to praise His Holy Name, because He is worthy to be praised!

Free the Trapped Soul

Any struggle is a desert because it involves loss. If our motivations are primarily useful, this loss may consist only in denial that you did it, not God's grace. Most of our deserts lie somewhere between these extremes, and most of the time we do little more than dance around the edges. All the same, deserts enrich our lives immeasurable. Each desert holds seeds of repentance, possibilities of recognizing how mixed our motives really are. And, with the rain of grace, each desert holds the possibility of our reclaiming out true heart's desire. Even if we only touch the edge, our desert teaches us about the limits of our personal power and points us towards that constant center of ourselves where our dignity is found in our dependence upon God.

Let us never forget that the deserts are gardens of courtship as well as fields of battle. Struggle with attachments can be seen as warfare with a devious enemy, or it can be seen as a romance in which the soul seeks the beloved for whom we thirst. Partly, this is simply a matter of attitude. In another sense, the transformation of desert into gardens is made possible only by God's grace raining upon the areas of our lives that are truly wastelands.

Chapter 11 Thank God for His Grace and Mercy

External or internal, chosen or not, the desert is characterized by a soul suffering from withdrawal symptoms, a mind and body deprived or false securities and therefore left to explore the mystical terrain of personal will power and Divine grace. At its mildest, the desert is a laboratory where one learns something about grace. In receiving God's grace, we are put in a testing ground where faith and love are tried by the fire. I am glad for God's grace, are you glad to be in God's grace, today?

Free the Trapped Soul

You have great potential!

God created you to be free, powerful, and filled with purpose.

You can and will experience a great intimacy with God. You can become a powerful instrument of His love and reconciliation, both to the Church and to a dying family seeking to find Christ.

We all have doubted God, our worth in His eyes, and our ability to know Him. As I, Gary Walker Jr., expound on the encouraging life story I lived and with God's help, and through faith in God. His love and purpose for me and you will be strengthened and your doubts will be dispelled. You may think of yourself as an ordinary person, but you have extraordinary potential. Unlock that potential today!

Very few believers choose to drift; seldom do Christians plan to be lukewarm. But poor performance undermines confidence, and failure causes discouragement. Temptation, even when we are overcomers, leaves us battle-scarred and weary. It is sometimes difficult to tell the difference between victory and defeat because issues are never clear-cut and our successes never total. When one has struggled through the testing time and finally endured, it seldom feels like triumph.

Chapter 11 Thank God for His Grace and Mercy

Someone has to help us at the time of our struggle. We need a brother in the hour of trial, and especially when we fail. Otherwise we fall into the discouragement of trying harder, or of never quite measuring up. The subtle shift from trust in Christ to our own self-efforts robs us of hope and joy. We begin to totally hurt, count disappointments and weigh sacrifices. And already the drift has set in. We need the warning, but more than that, we need to know that we are known, understood and loved by someone who has marked out our path, has won the victory and is with us on the way. That someone is Jesus. Every time you feel trapped, Jesus will free the soul.

Prayer

In the name of Jesus, I declare and decree the love of God over my life and those around me as I receive His guidance, correction and discipline. I will not operate as a normal Christian, but excel in charity (love). I commit my life and my ways to You, Lord God, and I know that You'll do exceedingly all I can ever ask, do or think.

May the Spirit of God give all understanding and wisdom, and may the sweet communion of the Holy Spirit, rest, rule and abide forevermore. Amen!

About the Author

Pastor Gary Walker Jr., is a resident of Annapolis, Maryland, and the eldest son of Gary Walker Sr. & Norma Jenkins both of Annapolis, Maryland. Always knowing he had a call on his life and knowing God was waiting for him to answer,. Pastor Gary Walker Jr. received his call to preach the Gospel in 2009. He is ordained under the Divine Leadership of Prophet Dewey Rowe, Ministries having pursued religious devotions and having given evidence of a divine call to the ministry according to the Gospel of St. Luke 4:18-19, and St. Matthew 28:18-20. Pastor Gary Walker Jr. has received several certificates in Theological Studies from Alpha Bible Institute, at the Glen Burnie campus of New Creation Deliverance Bible Way Church, of Glen Burnie, Maryland.

Pastor Gary Walker Jr. shares with his virtuous woman, Evangelistic Pastor Wannetta Ann Walker, Founder of No Division Ministries, Outreach. Together they share seven children and six grandchildren.

The mission for Pastor Gary Walker Jr., not liking himself to Paul, but is to travel the Damascus road experience and help those out of the by-ways and with God's help save souls and minister the Word of the True and Living God. He feels that if God can change him and save him from a burning hell, then the same God he serves can save and change you. He prays that you can use this, his experience in life, to see inside yourself to grow towards spiritual maturity and free the trapped soul within yourself.

www.ingramcontent.com/pod-product-compliance
Lightning Source LLC
Chambersburg PA
CBHW050438010526
44118CB00013B/1578